Yellow Umbrella Books are published by Capstone Press
151 Good Counsel Drive, P.O. Box 669, Mankato, Minnesota 56002
www.capstonepress.com

Library of Congress Cataloging-in-Publication Data
Endres, Hollie J.
What computers do / by Hollie J. Endres.
p. cm.
Summary: A simple introduction to the various ways in which people use
computers.
ISBN 0-7368-2941-5 (hardcover)—ISBN 0-7368-2900-8 (softcover)
1. Computers—Juvenile literature. [1. Computers.] I. Title.
QA76.23.E54 2004
004—dc21   2003008674

Editorial Credits
Editorial Director: Mary Lindeen
Editor: Jennifer VanVoorst
Photo Researcher: Scott Thoms
Developer: Raindrop Publishing

Photo Credits
Cover: Jon Feingersh/Corbis; Title Page: Don Farrall/PhotoDisc; Page 2: DigitalVision;
Page 3: Jim Cummins/Corbis; Page 4: Photodisc Green; Page 5: Steve Cole/PhotoDisc;
Page 6: SW Productions/PhotoDisc; Page 7: Tom and Dee Ann McCarthy/Corbis;
Page 8: DigitalVision; Page 9: Ed Bock/Corbis; Page 10: H. David Seawell/Corbis;
Page 11: Don Mason/Corbis; Page 12: Kevin R. Morris/Corbis; Page 13: Chris
Sorensen/Corbis; Page 14: AFP/Corbis; Page 15: Stockbyte; Page 16: Larry
Williams/Corbis

1 2 3 4 5 6 09 08 07 06 05 04

What Computers Do

by Hollie J. Endres

Consultant: Brian VanVoorst, Principal Research Scientist,
Honeywell Labs, Minneapolis, Minnesota

Yellow Umbrella Books

an imprint of Capstone Press
Mankato, Minnesota

What Computers Do

Computers are everywhere! But how do people use computers? What do computers do?

People use computers to hold and sort information.

00	94,000	164,000	13,
00	69,000	139,000	13,5
00	67,000	137,000	13,5
00	70,000	140,000	13,5
0	48,778	89,678	13,5
0	76,551	117,451	13,5
0	33,737	74,637	13,5
0	29,500	70,400	13,5

People use computers to do math problems. Computers can do math problems much faster than people.

Some computers are connected together. They can share information with one another.

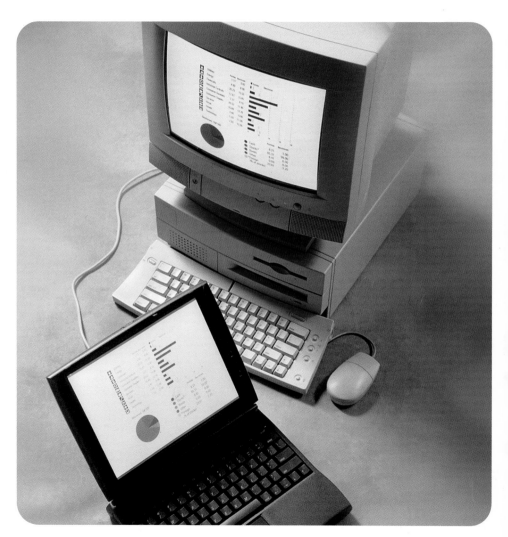

You can send a letter from
one computer to another.

You can use a computer to buy things without leaving home. The things you buy can be mailed to you.

Computers at Work

Many people use computers
for the work that they do.

Teachers use computers. Computers help their students learn.

Factory workers use computers.
Computers control machines
that do dangerous work.

Store owners use computers.
Computers help them keep
track of what they sell.

Scientists use computers.
Computers can draw pictures to
help them see how things work.

Pilots use computers. Computers tell pilots where to go and how high to fly.

Computers Every Day

Many things you use every day
have computers in them.
Computers help make them work.

Cars and microwave ovens have computers in them. Video games have computers, too!

Computers are everywhere!
Have you used a computer
today?

Words to Know/Index

Word Count: 186
Early-Intervention Level: 14

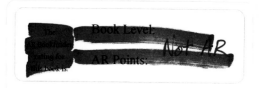